'The Other Way'?

The stories of lesbian and gay Christians are not often heard. This book contains the testimonies of fourteen lesbian and gay Anglicans, lay and ordained. The contributors come from evangelical and catholic backgrounds and describe journeys lived with courage, confidence, hope, determination and pain.

The stories recount the experience of reconciling sexuality and personal spirituality; the ways in which the pressure to deny homosexuality and marry have been resolved; the experience of calling, selection, training and ordination as a gay or lesbian; the damaging effects of inappropriate pastoral care; and the dignity, maturity and integrity that characterises the lives of many lesbian and gay Christians.

The book is offered as a contribution to the debate within the Church of England and as a resource for the 1998 Lambeth Conference.

Colin Coward is an Anglican priest, architect and psychotherapist who has worked in the parochial ministry for 17 years. He is Convenor of the Anglican Lesbian and Gay Clergy Consultation and the founder of *Changing Attitude*, a group dedicated to working within the Anglican Church for the affirmation of lesbian and gay Christians.

'The Other Way'?

Anglican Lesbian and Gay Journeys

Edited by

Colin Coward

CHANGING ATTITUDE

LONDON
1998

First published in Great Britain in 1998 by

CHANGING ATTITUDE
11 Murfett Close
Victoria Drive
Wimbledon
London SW19 6QB

A catalogue record for this book is available
from the British Library.

ISBN 0 9533678 0 0

Typeset in Monotype Sabon by
Strathmore Publishing Services, London N7

Printed and bound in Great Britain by
Ipswich Book Company, Ipswich, Suffolk

Contents

Contents

Foreword

The importance of this collection of personal testimonies has a lot to do with the way in which it challenges the idea that gay and lesbian Christians in the churches are somehow looking for an easy option. Whatever your views on the underlying issue, these reflections and recollections will make clear the cost and the integrity involved in living as a gay or lesbian person struggling to be loyal to the Christian tradition and the Christian community. Can this seriousness be received as a gift in our Church? This is the question these pages pose, gently but urgently.

THE RT REVD ROWAN WILLIAMS
Bishop of Monmouth

Preface

The majority of lesbian and gay members and clergy within the Church of England are at present invisible. Their stories are not known by their congregations and bishops and their experience is not available to the Church. The contributors to this book write often of their desire to live with integrity and honesty in a Church which demands secrecy and dishonesty. Being gay often creates a person who is more than usually aware of their feelings, empathetic and sensitive to the experience of others who carry what they believe to be shameful memories, thoughts and temptations. Lesbian and gay Anglicans *are already* a great gift to the Church. It is our hope that in telling our stories, you, the reader, will be left with a greater awareness of the experience, both positive and negative, of living and ministering in a Church which makes honesty about sexual identity so difficult for its lesbian, gay and bisexual members.

COLIN COWARD

Introduction

Is he 'the other way'?

This was one of the questions asked by gay men trying to discretely discover whether another man was homosexual in the years before law reform in 1967, and the advent of gay bars, discos, magazines, shops and a 'gay lifestyle'. Back then, a man who was 'the other way' was a man like me, gay, homosexual, bent, queer, a poof – the words used to identify me and those like me were mostly derogatory or offensive. Back then, for me, was the 1960s and 70s, when it was difficult to know where to go to meet other gay men, or how to identify them in a social environment. To deal with this problem, an alternative language had developed – Polare – with which gay men were able to communicate in a particularly sexual and explicit way. Those of you who used to listen to Julian and Sandy on *Round the Horne* will already be familiar with this mode of communication.

Many of the essays published here started life as testimonies given at the beginning of meetings of the Lesbian and Gay Clergy Consultation. Two or three members were asked in advance to talk for 5 minutes about their sexuality and how it had affected their vocation, selection process, college experience, ministry and spirituality. Those invited to contribute essays has expanded beyond this group to include lay as well as ordained testimonies.

The testimonies reveal a range of experiences which will be all too familiar to many lesbian and gay Anglicans, and especially to those who are ordained and working in the parochial ministry. Here, the anxiety about being gay and ordained is most strong. Clergy fear the way in which their congregation or bishop would react if they discovered they were gay. It isn't even that a priest needs to have a partner or to have ever been intimate with another man or woman. The message being given is that to be gay is in itself unacceptable and is emotionally difficult for the church to deal with.

As a result, individuals are driven to such extremes as the contemplation of suicide or the reality of a complete mental and emotional breakdown. Some gay clergy are fortunate enough to work in dioceses where their sexuality is known and understood by their bishops. Here, appropriate and often generous pastoral care may be given. Elsewhere, fear of their bishop's negative or hostile attitude, whether real or imagined, means that clergy have to keep the real reason for their distress secret and pretend nothing is wrong, or the reason for distress is something quite different. Sometimes, even when a bishop or the staff of a theological college is sympathetic, the most inappropriate and damaging reactions can occur.

A significant number of contributors have contemplated getting married in the hope that this will resolve their dilemma in a way which would make them more acceptable to the church; others have been or are married. Some marry knowing they are gay, others not even realising their true sexual identity at the time. Some marriages work well, others come to grief in a very painful separation and break up. This is another situation where the attitude of your bishop can be crucial in determining whether or not the reality of what is happening in a clergy marriage is understood. This can leave a wife or husband

and their children in as distressing and unsupported a place as their clergy partner.

All contributors have had to face the dilemma of whether or not to 'come out'. In the mind of every gay man or lesbian there can be an almost constant anxiety about whether to be secretive and hidden, or open and public about their sexuality. Behind the anxiety lies the question, how will this person or this group react to me if they *really* knew who I am. How would my churchwardens, my congregation, my colleagues, my bishop react? Would they approve or disapprove? Will I be safe, if I am a priest, will the information appear on my file, and how might this affect my move to a new parish or diocese? The disapproval and disgust expressed in parts of society and the church can become internalised into disgust with the self. Some essays reveal a person edging towards greater openness, knowing that there will be less to fear when they are truly out, both to themselves and in the world of the Church around them.

Some essays refer to the need to integrate body and spirit and to the essentially Incarnational, embodied experience of faith which is focused in the Eucharist, elemental, body and blood, body broken and integrated into our bodies and spirits. Lesbians and gays are not genitally obsessed in the way that those hostile to the physical expression of our sexuality seem to be. We *can* have a heightened awareness of the erotic, and work consciously to integrate erotic and physical awareness into our spirituality together with an emotional, affective spirituality and the often safer, more cerebral and intellectual Anglican mode.

The 20th Anniversary Service of the Lesbian and Gay

Christian Movement was perhaps the first time that a large number of lesbian and gay Christians gathered to worship in a very visible way. But large numbers of lesbian and gay Christians have been meeting regularly in the different Anglican and ecumenical groups which have evolved over the past 22 years. Some groups are primarily pastoral and supportive; others have a political agenda and are determined to confront the Church with the reality of its lesbian and gay members and our desire to find affirmation and acknowledgement of our presence and ministry within the Church.

The Clergy Consultation was founded in 1976 as a support organisation for gay and bisexual clergy and ordinands and their partners, at almost the same time as the Lesbian and Gay Christian Movement. A group of friends met and drew up a list of *their* friends who they thought might be gay, inviting them to a first meeting. Everything was done in a very subtle and unspoken way, though the assumption was that those who turned up were all 'the other way'. The group expanded through personal contact over the years until more than five hundred were on the Consultation mailing list. Numbers declined after the traumas of the Higton debate in General Synod in 1987, and following the decision to welcome ordained lesbians as members. Those male priests opposed to the ordination of women withdrew from the Consultation in large numbers. The national membership of the Consultation now stands at 200.

The group meets twice a year and has welcomed as guest speakers such figures as Bishops Bill Swing of California, Jack Spong and Rowan Williams, Chris Smith MP and Michael Vasey. More recently, meetings have been held with groups of Diocesan and Assistant Bishops including Roy Williamson, John Gladwin, Michael Bourke and Michael Scott-Joynt (representing the House of Bishop's Working Party on Human Sexuality), and a subsequent meeting with theological college and course staff members.

When the Consultation was founded, the climate of opinion towards such clergy within the church meant that they had to remain largely hidden and secretive. For many today, fear of homophobic attitudes within the church, real or imagined, means that it can still be difficult to be lesbian and gay and live easily with your sexuality and remain in the Church. The Consultation has offered such clergy an important network of support and encouragement through difficult times.

The Consultation operates a strict policy of confidentiality to protect the interests of members who fear the reaction of their Bishop, DDO, Archdeacon, colleagues, PCC or congregation to their sexuality. Most of these essays are being published anonymously for the same reason. Some of the contributors were willing to reveal their identity, but most were not. This is true even for those members whose bishops are fully aware of their sexuality and value and affirm their relationships, welcoming partners to diocesan events. Lesbian and gay clergy live with a high level of anxiety and fear. They fear being scapegoated and rejected, they fear loss of job and reputation, they fear the consequences of honesty when the search for a new parish in a different, less open and less accepting diocese begins.

The Consultation meets some of the needs of lesbian and gay clergy. Other organisations respond to the needs of lay lesbian and gay Christians, most notably the Lesbian and Gay Christian Movement (LGCM). Support and social contact is provided by over twenty-five local groups spread throughout England. Some groups lead a fragile, low-profile existence, and can be Anglican and male-dominated. Others have been in existence since LGCM was formed (one predates LGCM), and boast membership figures of over a hundred. The needs of evangelicals are met by the Evangelical Fellowship, and of lesbians by Lesbian Matters, which has over 400 members. Roman Catholic, Methodist and United Reformed Church members have their own caucuses and a Counselling Helpline offers confidential, professional support to those exploring their relationship with the Church, their spirituality and sexuality. Other denominations and groups have separate organisations – Quest in the Roman Catholic Church, the Quaker Lesbian and Gay fellowship, the Unitarian Gay Fellowship, Affirmation UK for Mormons and the Christian Science Lesbian and Gay group. The Metropolitan Community Church, founded in the United States and with congregations around the world, has a number of churches in the United Kingdom, and offers worship specifically but not exclusively for lesbian, gay and bisexual Christians. Kairos in Soho is a project based in Old Compton Street, the focus of London gay social life, and aims to meet deeper social and spiritual needs.

Lesbian and gay Anglicans in the Dioceses of London and Southwark benefit from support networks founded at a similar time five years ago in each diocese. The Southwark Network meets six times a year and has a membership of over a hundred. More recently, a Black

Lesbian and Gay Christian Fellowship was formed, meeting under the auspices of a Methodist Church in South London. Action for Gay and Lesbian Ordination (AGLO) is an organisation campaigning for the ordination of openly gay people in the Church of England.

Changing Attitude is a group of Anglican Christians who have been invited to make a presentation to the bishops of the Lambeth Conference meeting in Canterbury in the summer of 1998. There, we will tell our stories in the context of theological and biblical reflection. We hope that the bishops who listen to us will lay aside fear and prejudice and allow themselves to experience us as people called by God to full membership of the Church. We are loving, worshipping, faithful people, learning to live in intimate relationship with God, with ourselves, our partners, and with all who call themselves Christian. We are already fully a part of the one body which is Christ's Church. We hope this book will encourage many other lesbian and gay Christians to tell their stories, and the wider Church to listen with openness and respect.

COLIN COWARD
London, June 1998

1 Living in a climate of deception and dishonesty – practice makes perfect

Jeremy was born in 1940 and trained at the College of the Resurrection, Mirfield, before being ordained in 1968. He served as curate in two parishes in the north of England, as vicar of a city parish for 15 years, and has been vicar of his present parish since 1990.

I am a priest within the Church of England. I have ministered in parishes for over thirty years, and will soon celebrate the thirtieth anniversary of a permanent, committed partnership with another man. Those in authority would prefer to ignore, or even to deny, my existence – and the existence of a significant number of clergy like myself – to say nothing of the even greater number of lay men and women who are homosexual and try to live a Christian life. The Church can just about accept us if we remain celibate; she can cope with us if we confess the occasional misdemeanour and seek forgiveness; but if we are living in a relationship, then there are those who would have us hounded out of the Body of Christ. Most recently, this attitude has surfaced in the Kuala Lumpur Statement, which has been endorsed by the Forward in Faith Council as well as by Reform. Twenty years after the Gloucester Report, the Church of England seems to be no closer to resolving this debate – chiefly because it refuses to have a debate.

Archbishop William Temple declared that Christianity is the most materialistic of the world's religions: a gloss on the words from St John's Gospel: 'The Word was made flesh and dwelt among us.' It is therefore ironic that this same Christianity has found the flesh so difficult to handle. As someone pointed out, if only St Augustine had made an honest woman of his mistress, the Church's attitude to sex might have been very different. Instead, there has been a fear of human sexuality in general, and of homosexuality in particular. Yet the Judeo-Christian tradition is most true both to itself and to the Lord when it emphasises the unity of body and soul. In a real sense, we do not just have a body – each one of us is our body. All we are and all we seek to express has to be conveyed by means of our flesh and blood. Our sexual orientation is therefore an inevitable and a significant part of our life and our approach to daily living.

Each one of us treads this road of life trying to make sense of the way things are for us. We do not have to walk alone, because there is the common experience of human history for us to learn from. Christians also have the tradition of the Church as well as the words of Scripture. Each of us is a unique individual, precious in God's sight. I still pray for the day when the facts of my life and my track record may provide the proof that to be Christian and homosexual is not incompatible, nor can celibacy be compulsorily imposed upon all of us. How then do I come to terms with life, realising that I am not as most men are? Instead, I am one among a minority, albeit a significant one, which has been persecuted in most generations by both Church and state.

I have grown up this way, and can point to no incident which has 'made' me homosexual. No one has ever abused me or interfered with me. I can recall no time when I did not feel attracted to those of my own sex. I was not segregated from the female sex – all my schooling and student days from the age of five until twenty-three were spent in co-education. About the age of nineteen or twenty, the truth began to dawn upon me when I read this description of what it means to be homosexual; 'to be attracted towards men, in the way in which most men are attracted towards women'. I knew at once that this described my own deepest feelings. Several times I had dated women in the hope that something might click. It was a relief to understand that this side of life was closed to me. Even so, in those days before the 1967 reform act, I kept myself to myself, never frequenting any gay pubs or clubs. I saw my future as that of a confirmed bachelor, who would be dedicated to whatever work I undertook.

During my years as a teacher, my vocation to the priesthood returned. This was some relief, because here was a way of life which catered for the single state – I could be a priest or a religious, and not have to explain why I was not married and unlikely ever to be so. This ideal survived my years at theological college, but not my first year in a parish. Not for the first time I fell in love with another man, but, for the very first time, it was mutual. Hitherto, I had only had crushes on those who were in no position to reciprocate my feelings. In my late twenties, I found myself beginning a relationship which has been as close to marriage as is possible for two men devoted to each other. As with any relationship, there have been moments of difficulty and tension, but the partner-ship has flourished and we are both convinced that God has done more with us together that He could have done with either one of us separately. How can I reconcile my lifestyle with my own conscience, as well as with the teaching of the Bible and the tradition of the Church, both of which are usually cited in order to condemn any such homosexual relationship as being contrary to God's holy law?

How then can I live as I do, and still believe in the Bible? If homosexual orientation as we know it was unknown to the writers and editors of the Scriptures, then it is quite possible to argue that a permanent, faithful, committed relationship between two men or two women is compatible with the teaching of the Bible. God and his Truth are not confined within the covers of the Bible, and if the Holy Spirit guides us not just to read the words of scripture, but also to read between the lines, then it is reasonable to see homosexual partnerships as part of God's purpose for some people.

How do I reconcile my lifestyle with the tradition of the Church? Once again, I appeal to the work of the Holy Spirit, leading us into a fuller understanding of God's Truth as revealed in Jesus Christ. Tradition is not only something handed on, but also something that has to be received by each generation and interpreted in ways which each generation can understand. Tradition can therefore develop, and our modern understanding of homosexual orientation need not be seen as contrary to the Church's tradition.

When the Gloucester Report was published in 1979, I had great hopes that this would lead to a reasoned debate at all levels in the Church, from parish discussion groups and PCC's right up to General Synod. The report was shelved, and the issue was not faced. Nor did the General Synod face it in November 1987 when the

Reverend Tony Higton's motion sparked off a debate which has since led to the very kind of witch-hunt he denied he was seeking.

Nor has this situation been redeemed by the House of Bishop's document *Issues in Human Sexuality*. This has been interpreted by opposing camps according to their own preferences. 'There is no fear in love, but perfect love casts out fear' (1 John 4.18). The present climate in the Church of England is casting out that perfect love which is possible for homosexual partnerships as for heterosexual marriages. There remains a climate of deception and dishonesty among Bishops and their clergy as all attempt to present a respectable face to the world. This is hardly the way that Christ's Family should behave. Were the Church brave enough to offer an ethic for homosexuals which emphasises the fulfilment to be found in permanent, faithful, committed relationships, then this would indeed be a heaven-sent relief for many of God's sons and daughters. People like myself are caught in a situation from which we cannot escape. Meanwhile, we have to keep our heads down, and try to minister in Christ's name as if we were the ordinary, heterosexual beings that both Church and society would like us to be.

I want to claim that by the grace of God I am a good priest *because I am homosexual*, and not in spite of it. My faithful commitment to a partner allows me to sympathise more readily with the bereaved at funerals, because I could imagine how I would feel if my partner had died. I can rejoice with those seeking to be married, because I myself know what a joy it is to be wholly committed to another human being. There are moments, of course, when all is not sweetness and light, but such occasions can be faced and lived through, and then the relationship can emerge wiser and stronger from the experience. This is not to deny that there is a place for celibacy, but that has to remain a vocation to which some are called, and never become a condition that is imposed on anyone. Because I am homosexual and have a partner God can work through the two of us in a more fruitful way than if we had not been so committed to Him and to each other.

There are too many gay clergy and lay people who have got married in the hope that this would somehow prove to be a 'cure'. All too often, these are the ones who fall foul of the law in public toilets. Gay priests who are unwilling or unable to live in permanent relationships must suffer, unless they can positively commit themselves to celibacy and find a support group. While matrimony and celibacy are recognised states within the Church, those of us who are homosexual have to fend for ourselves. Support groups do exist, but these are necessarily unofficial and secret. The failure to provide any ethic for gay Christians leaves them with no meaningful guidelines.

Churchmanship also has tragic effects upon both extremes, Catholic and Evangelical. Until recently when a support group was formed, Evangelical gay clergy were far worse off than their Catholic counterparts because Protestantism has rarely accorded any place to the single state, and never accepted homosexual behaviour. On the Catholic wing, there can also be intolerance. Traditional moral theology has been able to cope with those who confess their sins – thus it has been possible to live a life of one-night stands and fleeting relationships, each of which is repented of and confessed, whereas those who seek to maintain permanent and faithful partnerships are totally condemned. There can also be hostility from those clergy who have married to cure or camouflage their own sexual preferences, and they can be very loud in condemning those who are enjoying what they themselves might have preferred.

My greatest frustration is that I cannot share the fact of my love with those among whom I minister. Many may guess, a chosen few actually know, most would probably accept me and my partner for what we are. In the Church of England, as well as in England, homosexuality still remains 'the love that dare not speak its name'. I am vulnerable in a way that touches the very heart of my being, and this can be distressing. There is always a fear that I may be victimised within the very institution that ought to be able to accept me as I am for God's sake. If only I could make my relationship more widely known and show that it is possible to be Christian and gay, then many others in the Church and in the wider community could be comforted, and there might be less prejudice and victimisation. The figure of the scapegoat may be very close to the person of Jesus, but Christians today have enough to bear in his Name, without being persecuted because their sexual orientation does not meet with the approval of the majority in the Church and State.

In my relationship I have consciously tried to imitate what is required for a successful marriage, while recognising that a gay partnership cannot be equal to that. I believe that it is a fundamental and God-given characteristic of human nature that each one of us is created for the ideal of a one-to-one partnership. Homosexual pairing therefore needs to be committed, permanent and faithful as any marriage aims to be. Yet the Church as a whole will not consider even this restricted view as a basis for an ethic for gay Christians. I owe a lot to the stability which such a relationship can bring, as well as to the happiness and fulfilment it provides.

How will the Church ever know what it is like to be a Christian, a priest, and gay, unless it asks me and all the others like me? Our experience and our loves are the evidence the Church needs in order to reconcile the way we are with the Way of Christ. When there is a climate of opinion that allows us to speak for ourselves without fear of victimisation, then and only then will the Church be able to formulate some kind of ethic and theology for homosexual men and women.

2 Being the truth – is speaking the truth

Bill was born in Canada in 1927. Having arrived in England, he followed a career in nursing, working at higher levels of management. He trained with the Southwark Ordination Course and at Salisbury Theological College, and was ordained as an NSM in 1970. He founded Reaching Out, a listening centre, in 1979, and since 1982 has worked largely with gay men living with the challenges of HIV and AIDS.

'Speaking the truth in love' is the way for all who have been baptised into 'ways' of Jesus. The Christian vocational responsibility is to be the truth of our lives, lives nurtured by the gifts of co-creative loving, whether we are being procreative or not and whatever our sexual orientation. I am fully aware that many priests who are homosexuals feel they are not in truth accepted by their bishop (unless they are celibate). My experience with four diocesan bishops and four area bishops has been just the opposite. My being a priest who happens to be homosexual is not a problem for me and nor has it been, so far as I know, for any of these bishops.

Working as I have been since my ordination with young persons, the homeless, those who are chemical and alcohol abusers and with young men involved in the sex industry at street level, it seemed right that I should inform the bishops of my sexual orientation. If this information caused them any anxiety, I am not aware of it. All have been very supportive of me in these various ministries and my orientation has not been a problem in the different parishes I have been associated with.

My question is, if I can be accepted as a priest who happens by the grace of God to be homosexual, why do so many other bishops find it such a problem to cope with other priests who are gay? Bishops are supposed to be our 'Fathers in God' but many live in fear of the sexuality of their gay priests. It is this fear that is the very basis of homophobia. Within the Church there seems to be no other prejudice quite like it, nurtured as homophobia is by the fear of closed minds and hearts.

Since 1983 I have been pastorally involved with many who are living with the challenge of HIV/AIDS. They frequently live in long-standing relationships where the caring for one another is nurtured by their friendship of love. These co-creative partnerships deny all the negative assumptions that have been and are still being made by the churches. It is because of these experiences that I find myself asking why?, why the discrepancy between the church's official statements and reports about homo-sexuality over the years and the growing climate of accep-tance of the gay priest or minister by many local parishes, who daily experience their ministry as part of the continuing ministry of the Church of God.

The Revd Simon Bailey in a Sunday sermon to his congregation asks 'What is it that makes us so anxious to lay down laws for other people's lives – especially their private sexual lives? Why do we so completely fail to trust them to have consciences of their own? Why on earth do we believe that pronouncements of the church will make the slightest difference except to harden peo-ple's attitudes to an increasingly moralistic institution?

There is some deep seated and disturbing insecurity in us, an insecurity about our own identity and our own behaviour that makes us want to legislate for others, to dictate how they must behave even in private – we hanker for a power over others that we don't have ourselves.... This does not remove from the church any role in discussing and guiding morality though it does basically alter the approach. We cease to lay down laws and declare ourselves 'not like other men', rather in this way we join with the 'wounded surgeon' who knows how to heal because he is wounded himself....' He ended, 'The new radically free Christian behaviour is best summed up in the stark, glad, risky freedom of St Augustine's phrase, 'Love and do as you like.' 'The first and over-riding principle in Christian morals is not the making of clear rules and sharp dividing lines – the first principle is "No condemnation" – Christianity is not about guilt, but about this sigh of relief – "not condemned" knowing that we find ourselves free to set about making that good life, living better.' [1]

Clearly (and sadly) gay men and lesbian women are being forced to suffer, to live out what is essentially the Church's problem of failure to totally accept what is by nature normal for gay men and women. It is a failure to accept us as we are members of the community of *all* God's people like everyone else. Within the history of Christianity there have been times when such relationships were accepted. Today we are becoming increasingly aware of the fact that many within the Church, as in the wider community, were born to be attracted to others of the same sex. Therefore it is imperative that the Church, nurtured by the courage of truth, openly supports and indeed blesses such co-creative partnerships rather than causing them to be hidden and lied about.

For this to occur in truth, the Church must let go of its deep suspicion of the body and its negative obsessions with sexuality, so often portrayed as *the* potential danger to a person's eternal salvation and eternal growing. It is time that religion ceased presenting the body as the source of evil, ambiguity, lust and seduction. There is no doubt in my mind that it is how we feel about ourselves that determines the way we express our sexuality, including heterosexuality, homosexuality, bisexuality and celibacy.

I am convinced that sex, sexuality, sensuality and spirituality are all intrinsically linked.

Sex is a biologically based need oriented to co-creation, procreation, pleasure and tension release.

Sexuality is a more comprehensive term associated with more diffuse and symbolic meanings and psychological and cultural orientations.

Sensuality has to do with sensations like touching, smelling, tasting, hearing and seeing. It is a bridge between being sexual and being spiritual.

Spirituality has to do with unity – soul with soul, soul with body, person with person, creation with co-creativeness, sacred with secular, masculinity with femininity, compassion with justice, life with death and death with life.

I believe we should not be afraid of our differing sexualities. They are the raw material of holiness. What Jesus the Christ has not assumed in his total self, he has not healed. Our bodies are for the embodying of our loving, one to another. It is impossible to love ourselves or others if we deny the value of our bodies, the temple of the soul and its sensuality. To repress the sensual, the spiritual wonder in our lives, including the erotic and ecstatic experiences (i.e. our embodied spiritual experiences) is to destroy our innate capacity for recognising and welcoming the divine mystery within.

Due to the theological misinterpretation of certain passages in the Old and New Testaments many men and women are being forced to live in the dark shadow of fear when they wish to live in the light of love's nurturing. Reconciliation between the theology of fear and love is essential. This means that the Church must dare to look beyond labels. In God, the only label, if it is such, is that of son or daughter – 'This is my beloved Son, this is my beloved Daughter, in whom I take delight.' Once we start looking beyond any label we shall recognise and rejoice in the fact that the peoples of God are beautiful, whatever their sexual orientation or gender, wearing as they do, however imperceptibly and imperfectly, the multi-coloured rainbow cloak of God.

I query how many bishops and others have made any attempt really to get to know men and women who are either homosexual or lesbian who are living wholesome and co-creative lives alongside others, contributing much within the various ministries of the Church and the community. I get the impression that many who condemn same gender partnerships are not interested in the whole person, but in genitalia and what they assume is done with it. In so doing, they are condemning men and women to the peripheries of the Church. 'You are welcome if you come on our terms' excludes those with whom Jesus socialised and for whom he died. It is crucial for the Church to be the truth and not to continue to be blinkered by a fear that prevents so many from accepting the truth of St Paul's statement to the Galatians: 'there is neither Jew nor Greek, slave or free, male or female; for you are all one in Christ Jesus.' (Galatians 3:28, NIB).

Speaking the truth in love demands being the truth in love. We may need to remind ourselves of Pontius Pilate's question to Jesus and ask as did Meister Eckhart, 'What is truth? Truth is something so noble that if God could turn aside from it, I would keep to the truth and let God go.' – (from *The Fragments* [2]).

[1] Bailey, Rosemary, *Scarlet Ribbons: A priest with AIDS*. Serpent's Tail, 1997
[2] Eckhart, Meister, *Sermons and Treatises*, Vol. III, translated and edited by M. O'C. Walshe. Element Books, 1987

3 The tragedy of Church and college pastoral care

Helen was born in 1963, and after a career in the per-forming arts trained at a catholic theological college. She was ordained in 1996, is married, and is a Senior Curate in the south of England.

I grew up in a small northern town where the culture was very homophobic. Consequently I never dared to think about my sexuality in my teens. It wasn't until I left home and joined a lay community in London that I came to terms with the whole of who I was. In our community we had prayer together twice daily, mostly of a contemplative nature. While I found the silence very nourishing there was a sense that something wasn't quite right for me. I felt as though I wasn't in a proper relationship with God.

That was until I met Claire. I realised one day that I had fallen in love with this woman, and it really was like being hit with a thunderbolt. I wanted to sing from the rooftops – I felt so alive and so full of happiness. I realised that my relationship with God had changed too. Suddenly the contemplative prayer of the community was different, it became all absorbing. I realised that the struggles I'd had with prayer before were because I hadn't been honest with God. I really believe that God created me to be a lesbian, and I know that once *I* had accepted who I was, and, more importantly promised to be true to who I was and not run away, my life had an integrity about it that I had not known before.

I am sure that had I not recognised the gift God had given me in my sexuality, I would not be a priest today. For if I could not have accepted the call to be me, how could I possibly have even heard the call to priesthood, never mind been able to respond.

Both Claire and I went on to train for ordination together. During my first few months at theological college, I considered myself very fortunate, both to be in a stable and loving relationship with another woman (also an ordinand at the same college as me), and to have the support of many in the college (including staff) for that relationship. My partner and I were always open about our relationship, believing that a double life is neither honest nor healthy. We were also fortunate in that around twenty per cent of ordinands in our college were fairly openly gay, lesbian or bisexual, so we were never really out on a limb as a result of our sexuality. The college was comparatively gay-friendly – so much so that it publicly allowed the formation of a LesBiGay support group.

Unfortunately, that support dropped away dramatically when my partner ended our relationship. Whereas we had been able to be quite open about the relationship (holding hands in public, dancing together intimately at college parties, being invited out as a couple, etc.), I suddenly discovered that discussing our break-up was not to be tolerated. As I am the kind of person who needs to talk through emotions with another, being forbidden to do this had terrible consequences for me. Not only did I begin to fall apart psychologically, finding study impossible, but I became physically ill too, so much so that I ended up almost unable to move – literally crippled by unexpressed grief and loss.

After two weeks I was summoned by the principal and told that my behaviour was unacceptable and had to stop. He was uninterested in the reason why I was falling apart and the fact that I had been told I mustn't talk about the relationship break-up. I was then told I was being sent away to a convent where 'I would sort my life out'. After this I was sent to the tutor in spirituality who would help me find a suitable place to go. I said I didn't want to go away but needed my friends around me. The reply was that this wasn't about what *I* wanted or needed. I was simply to do as I was told. I returned to my room feeling worse than ever.

Two days later I was sent for again and told to pack a bag as I would be going away that afternoon. It was suggested that I should leave discretely, not saying goodbye to anyone, and not telling anyone where I was going. It was pointed out that whilst at the convent I *would* talk to the chaplain, and he *would* report back to the principal. Thus I was sent away to the middle of nowhere for one month to live with nuns whom I had never met before in my life.

Fortunately the chaplain was rather more pastoral and prayerful than my college principal, and refused to pass on anything of our conversations to the college. With the love and care of the chaplain and the nuns I was able to begin to rebuild my life slowly and painfully, so that I could at least return to college after the month away and resume my studies. It didn't make it any easier to see my former partner in chapel every day, but through the prayerful support of the convent I found enough emotional strength to get me through my final months at college.

I also found the courage to ask myself whether I still

wanted to be ordained and to belong to a church that could treat people so appallingly. I came to the conclusion that I could do no other since this is what God had called me to. I was ordained and am now extremely happy and fulfilled in parish ministry. However, whilst I am convinced that what I am doing is right, I also know that God has called me to work for the Kingdom and not just for the Church of England. If the time should come when I can be a more effective priest outside the Church of England then I hope I will have the courage to go wherever God calls me.

As I reflect on my experiences at college, and particularly the lack of support at a time when I so needed support, I find myself wondering how the college would have handled the marriage break-up of a heterosexual couple. I doubt they would have been told they mustn't discuss it with others in the college. They would probably have been offered counselling, told that as members of one community we were all there to help one another, and encouraged to talk it through. I doubt whether one of them would have been sent away into exile so things could settle down. They would probably have been offered all the support the college could give them.

For a Church that is supposed to be living out the Gospel and proclaiming the unconditional love of God as revealed in Jesus, I find it tragic that a college preparing men and women to be ministers of that Church was so incapable of teaching by example and showing me the love and care that I needed when I was at my most broken and vulnerable.

4 A welcome home

David is 49 and trained as a teacher before returning to university to read theology at Nottingham. His background is evangelical, and he was ordained in 1983, serving his title in a suburban parish. Following five years as Vicar of a middle-class urban parish, in 1991 he moved to a parish with a more cosmopolitan character.

There have been many times when I've wondered whether I'd have become a Christian at all if I'd been heterosexual. Certainly, my experience of God's grace could not have been the same if I'd been part of the heterosexual mainstream. My return to faith as an adult was entirely the result of another man falling in love with me. That is how God worked in me.

My parents had sent me to Sunday school, and as a teenager I had found church to be a good experience. I was in the choir and enjoyed it very much. My confirmation was an enormously moving event. I can still remember it and the feeling of closeness to God that surrounded it. I don't recall in my formative years that anyone preached about homosexuality or denounced it, but I sensed it was something the Church condemned. By my mid-teens I knew that I was gay. It wasn't a traumatic discovery or one I felt I had to fight or seek advice about. It wasn't the result of sexual experimentation with others. I wasn't at boarding school or any other context where such things might happen. At seventeen I was still too young to distinguish what the Church thought about people like me from what God might think. I couldn't deny who I was, so I let go of God and spent ten years feeling atheist and agnostic by turns. It wasn't that I had to choose between conventional morality and a wild gay lifestyle. I said nothing to anybody and did nothing with anybody either.

I went through university and a couple of years of voluntary work overseas and then settled to a teaching career. John was one of my colleagues. We got on very well and our friendship flourished but it never crossed my mind that he might be gay. Tentatively, and after we'd known each other for over a year, he told me he was in love with me. A year further on, we set up house together. That was in the mid-1970s, and we are still a couple now.

The fact that someone had fallen in love with me and was willing to commit himself to me opened me up to an understanding of the love of God that had been quite beyond me up to that point. John was a Christian for whom the question of ordination had been around in the past and was to come to fruition a few years later. We talked about faith and he pushed Christian books my way. The moment of conversion was quite sudden. We were out walking on the Sussex Downs one summer afternoon. There was a small, isolated church on the route and I slipped inside. Quite unexpectedly, I found myself on my knees, praying. My whole experience of life was transformed from that point. We joined our local church, and seven years later I was ordained.

At first I used to think of my sexuality as only one aspect of my personality, almost as if I was living and ministering as a Christian in spite of the fact that I was gay and in a gay relationship. It was increasingly obvious, though, that the reverse was true. In reality the gospel was so powerful and dynamic for me because of my experience of being part of a minority group who, at least until recently, have been looked down on and derided by the majority. Whatever sensitivity I have as a pastor comes not in spite of who I am but because of it. John has been a gift of God's grace to me, not just in bringing me to faith in the first place but in the context of a continuing relationship through which we grow. Without him I would have remained a mere shadow of my present self. Most husbands and wives would rejoice to say the same about their marriage, and I long for the day when the Church can affirm the creativeness and spiritual fruitfulness of a relationship like ours.

There is much pain in having to remain hidden. I am increasingly aware as the years go by of the price I have had to pay for remaining secretive about my true identity and from not being able to be open about John. There is a guardedness which spills over into my ministry and which I increasingly realise puts up a barrier between me and my congregation. I am on the road to openness about myself because I am sure that Christian living requires honesty and integrity, and because I am sure that honesty and integrity are vital ingredients for spiritual growth in the Christian community. When John fell in love with me I discovered, as if for the first time, what it meant to be loved, and I was suddenly able to respond to the love of God who opened his arms to me through John and welcomed me home.

5 Learning to be honest with myself and others

Rupert was born in 1944. After a career in chartered accountancy, he went to Salisbury Theological College and was ordained in 1971. He served his title in a London suburban church, was a university chaplain for 5 years, and an incumbent in an inner city parish for 16 years before moving 3 years ago to a large post-war estate.

I have prayed ever since I can remember, but it wasn't until I went to prep school that corporate religious experience became important for me. My first awareness of being sexual occurred around the age of 6, and I can remember my father's embarrassed attempt one Sunday morning to give me a sex talk. Before I went to public school my mother warned me about things other boys might want to do to me. I hadn't a clue what she was on about, but it fostered a sense of shame. At school there was occasional and innocent sexual exploration between boys and it was here that I was confirmed an Anglican. I have been a regular communicant ever since. A few of us used to get up early on Sunday and go to the local Anglican Church and I was part of a small group of boys who read the scriptures together early in the morning before school started.

By the time I left school all my sexual experience was in my head – I had no experience of sexuality in a relationship. I did not think of myself as gay, but thought that it was just a matter of one day meeting the right girl. The only problem was that I never seemed able to relate to a girl in the depth that I could with my best male friends. At school I had always had a special friend. My life at this point was very partitioned.

My faith was very important to me and it was really in the Eucharist that I felt most loved and accepted by God as I was. An expression of my faith was to become a voluntary helper at a youth club run by the Old Boys of my School. It was here that I made some really good Christian friends amongst the women and men leaders of the club and through them I was introduced to Lee Abbey, a Christian Community which ran a holiday centre for evangelism and renewal. I started going and taking a group from the club with me each year.

I attended Edinburgh University and during that time became very involved in the Anglican Chaplaincy. I was troubled by my sexuality and very briefly talked to the chaplain. He was kind and said it was just a phase many people went through. I didn't tell him very much and kept my doubts about his prognosis to myself. This was a slightly better attempt to talk to someone than the time when, aged 18 I went to see the Doctor about my problems. I only got as far as the front gate of the surgery and then walked away. I desperately needed to talk to someone, but just couldn't.

Following an unsuccessful attempt to change career I had another week at Lee Abbey and in praying and thinking about why things hadn't worked out, I began to wonder whether God had something else in store for me – indeed whether I was being called to the priesthood.

I felt very strongly (indeed heard a voice tell me) that I wasn't ready at this stage to know what God had in store for me, but that if I came back and joined the community when I had qualified as an accountant, I would find out. I qualified and was only reminded of the solemn promise that I had made to myself of joining the community when I attended a teaching week being run by a Cowley Father.

I was doing well in the accountancy firm and saw my faith working itself out in the business world and with the youth club in Lambeth. My promise continued to niggle me and I soon realised I had to get it out of my system. I negotiated six months' leave of absence from work to go down to Lee Abbey. It was a very formative period for me. Living in community usually makes you face yourself. In going there I had an additional unvoiced item on my agenda – of hoping to meet a girl, fall in love and get married.

It didn't happen. I fell in love with a male member of the community, and it was not reciprocated. However he put me in touch with the local vicar and arranged for me to make my first confession. I had been thinking about doing this for about two years and finally I got the push that was needed. It was very traumatic for me – the first time in my life that all the different compartments of my life were opened up to one person. This was the beginning of my coming to terms with my sexual orientation. Although I didn't welcome the realisation, I was gradual-ly coming to see that along with the part of myself that I hated, were some special gifts of sensitivity. By the end of my six months I knew that I had to change direction in my life.

I gave in my notice, went back to Lee Abbey for a fur-ther three months and had then to an ACCM selection conference. I arrived at Salisbury Theological College in the Michaelmas term of 1968. Salisbury was a lively and exciting place to be. The Principal was gay, and extremely kind and supportive to gay students. The college had a great sense of community and a culture of acceptance and support between gay and married students.

During the vacations I worked in hospitals in London. My new confessor suggested I stayed in one of the clergy houses for my other vacations. My first relationship was with the curate of this church. We were together for three years and are still good friends although we broke up during my first curacy. Following the break-up I became rather depressed. My training vicar asked me if I was all right and in the end I decided to tell him everything, as I felt honesty was important. Unfortunately it turned out to be information he found hard to handle. Everything I touched started to be wrong. I would be called round to his study and sooner or later the conversation would return to the issue I thought I had raised in confidence, and didn't really want to talk further about.

It was an extremely difficult time for both of us and we both developed health problems. My spiritual director and confessor met my vicar to try and help. If anything it made matters worse. Pressure was being put on me to leave the parish, although I felt strongly I was meant to serve my title there. In the end I agreed to go and see the Bishop. I knew his stance in these matters – 'what you do in private and is not a public matter is not of my concern'. I have never agreed with this, although I can see its administrative advantages. I therefore agreed to go and see the area Bishop. He was interested in meeting me because he was writing something on the subject at the time. The Bishop and I discussed what the church expected of me.

His line was not too different from *Issues in Human Sexuality*. Everything was OK as long as there was no genital expression.

I had met Peter, an American who was working in a local therapeutic community. I fell very strongly in love and we started a relationship. For me the crux of the matter was whether it was right or not for me to love another man – that Peter and I should belong together and be able to say 'we'. We were both in our twenties, I was deeply committed to him and physical closeness felt so comforting and right. I asked the Bishop what he expected me to do with my sexuality. He rather weakly said it must be very difficult. This talk seemed to pave the way for my ordination as a priest, and for my staying in the parish.

I left my first curacy with a great sense of love and respect for my first boss, which I think was reciprocated by him. My next appointment was as a university chaplain in part of London University. Peter and I lived together for five years in the top flat of a huge London vicarage. Our flat became a place of hospitality to many students and Peter came to be known and loved by many people in the chaplaincy.

Over the years I have taken part in a lot of compulsive/addictive therapeutic and self-help growth groups. Peter also had problems, and these came to a head with the illness of his Father back in the States. Peter went home to be with his father for six months, and on his return was drinking heavily. I was coming to see that I was also part of his problem. After his father's death Peter started being very destructive to himself.

This was an extremely painful time for both of us and

it became more than apparent to me that it would be impossible for us to live together in an ordinary vicarage without there being a scandal. I was finding it difficult to cope with him, and started attending Al-Anon twelve-step groups where I gained enough strength to move to a new appointment as Rector of an inner city South London Parish. Peter returned to the States. The break-up of our relationship was particularly painful, but we always remained in touch, and especially so over the last years of his life.

After a year in my new parish, I started a relationship with a member of the congregation, and we are still together after 18 years. We have never lived together, but do have a shared cottage in the country where we are known as a couple in the local rural community. Over the years an increasingly large group of people in the congregation came to know about our relationship. It was never an issue, as they knew us as people first. In the occasional sermon I had raised the issues surrounding homosexuality, and people were aware of where I stood, although they might not all have agreed.

In 1993 my situation became public. Graffiti daubed on the back of an advertising hoarding next door to the church, in full view of the block of flats facing it, read 'Rupert is gay, a big fat puff'. I was reading a book at the time about Martin Niemoller and his description of the experience of the Jews in Germany in the 1930s was fresh in my mind – how graffiti started appearing on their shops, how the Christians did not stand by them in solidarity, how Jews started changing their names, and how the persecution increased. As soon as I saw the graffiti, I knew I was not going to rub it off, and that I would preach about it the next day in church. I was nervous, but felt strangely empowered. I shared some of my feelings about graffiti in general, about how it affected the Jews in the '30s, and how it affects black people today. I then told them about the graffiti on the other side of the church's wall and what it said. I told them how I had wondered why people should do such things and also that it was demonstrably untrue. Shocked silence then turned to guffaws of laughter and relief as I followed it with 'I am not fat!'.

I asked people what they would do if the graffiti had been written about a black member of our congregation. Would we have just said sorry? Or would we have gone back together and in solidarity with him or her washed it off, possibly even taking photographs and writing to the newspaper stating that together we would fight the evil of racism and discrimination in whatever form it might take. The graffiti was still there the following Sunday, at which point two members of the congregation painted over it.

For the last three years I have been working as a vicar in a very large 'outer estate' parish on the edge of my diocese. During this time I have found it increasingly important to be more out and up front. The Twentieth Anniversary service of the Lesbian and Gay Christian Movement at Southwark Cathedral was an opportunity for this, and was a tremendously moving and empowering experience. I wrote about it in the Parish Magazine and had only one hate call, and lost one subscriber to the magazine.

I have tried to play my part in lobbying my diocesan contingent of General Synod. The letters I received in reply were interesting, varied and sometimes profoundly moving. From my understanding of family systems and how a local church operates, I am beginning to see how the wider church dumps much of its anxiety around sex on their 'delinquent' gay and lesbian brothers and sisters. By having an identifiable and vulnerable group which is perceived as having a sex problem, many members of the wider church are spared having to look at their own sexual problems and anxieties.

I want the church to affirm aspects of sexuality for straight and gay people alike – that it is a gift of God and that our sexuality finds its fulfilment within a relationship of commitment. It should be nurturing, tender, honest and not abusive. For many the integration and making whole of our sexuality can take a very long time. The church is seen as being hypocritical and unreal to people's experience. Fear and anxiety drive this charade, a potent cocktail, which will only be changed by those living honestly, lovingly and willing to suffer for the truth.

My partner and I are both very conscious of the support we receive from families and friends who love and support us as a couple. We have more heterosexual friends in this category than gay ones. It is always a pleasure to stay with them as a couple and know that it isn't a big issue. The major part of my life has been spent trying to be a faithful, honest and loving parish priest. My relationship gives me so much that undergirds my ministry. I believe my own priesthood has a greater integrity and power, the more I am able to be more honest both with myself and others.

6 An unsafe place to be

Jane was born in 1958 and has spent most of her years as a Christian in a strongly evangelical environment. She now worships with her partner and values an increasingly rich form of liturgy.

I think I was 10 years old when I started to realise I was different. I just didn't have those crushes on boys in the class. It was all a mystery to me. Instead, I looked longingly at other girls. With them, I wanted something more than friendship. On the outside I was a fun-loving, outgoing, extrovert but inside I was in great pain. It was lonely where I was. I was different and I thought nobody would understand. Once or twice I tried to talk to friends about this wickedness inside me and the extreme shame I felt, but it was hopeless.

I focused a lot of time and energy on the church, which felt a safe place to be. It helped me to block out the pain. I attended twice each Sunday and sang in the choir. I loved the processions and ritual and I felt safe with older people. Then I met Jeremy. This was my first major breakthrough in affirming my growing identity as a gay woman. We were in the same class at school. At first, we thought we felt for each other and had a brief time of 'going out' together. However, that soon fell apart. Some months later he told me he was having a relationship with another man. It was then that I told him I was gay too. It was an incredible feeling – I felt euphoric. We developed a close bond, sharing jokes and talking about who we fancied. Looking back, it was my first experience of gay community. His boyfriend was a lot older, rather rich (at least he seemed so to two teenagers) and used to take us to gay clubs. It was there that I first saw two girls kiss. It was an incredible moment for me. I felt the unbelievably powerful desire for that kind of intimacy which was never to leave me.

When I was 18 I left home and moved north to University. I was ready to move and looked forward to a new life and independence. In the very first days of term I found myself drawn to the University Christian Union – they seemed like a nice bunch of people. I had always had a faith in God and they did too – though they were rather more enthusiastic than I was used to! I went to a few of their meetings and before long was being drawn into the life of the group. I was invited to meals galore and was never short of friends. I attended regularly and felt very good.

Then, the axe fell. It became apparent that they were against homosexual practice. Up to this point I was probably very naive. I wasn't sexually active myself, but to have a relationship with a woman was very much part of my inner desires. During my friendship with Jeremy I had reached a greater sense of acceptance of my sexuality. I was even enjoying it. When I realised what my new-found Christian friends thought, however, I accepted their view without question. The group dynamic was so powerful and the sense of belonging engendered among this group so close that I accepted their view as right. It was also indicative of where I was – what I wanted so much I also feared deep down. I accepted their views as a defence against myself. During those first weeks of belonging to the CU I had powerful experiences of God that changed my sense of self. I loved myself for the first time in my life. I felt happy. I could look at the world and feel good instead of feeling I had to hide. So, when I heard their view on homosexuality I thought that was what God wanted me to do – reject my sexuality and choose him instead. Perhaps this was my cross and I had to bear it. Little did I know the effect it would have on my whole emotional life.

Life throughout my University years was dominated by my Christian faith. I became a prominent member of the CU, being President for a year. But all the time I was painfully aware of my longing for women, a longing that would not go away. I knew God's healing in other areas of my life but not with my sexuality. I prayed and prayed – I tried every trick in the book – but still the conflict remained; I was at war within my soul.

Just before leaving University I struck up a relationship with Michael, another gay man. We knew each other and had spent many hours talking about our common struggles. I think we were both lonely. Everyone else was pairing off, so why not us? We started having a relationship. I thought I had fallen in love with him. So, this was how God was going to heal us! This relationship went on for a year and marriage was on the horizon. Thank goodness he had the courage to call it off. It lacked that special spark and underneath we both knew why.

At this time I moved south to begin work and got involved in a big evangelical church. I was a house group leader, preached regularly and was seen as someone who was concerned for evangelical orthodoxy. My creed was that evangelicalism was good and liberalism was evil. I tried to focus my life wholly on God. I worked for a Christian organisation and was an activist, but I still kept falling in love with women and the desire for intimacy with a woman remained strong. I felt as if there was still a gaping hole in my life. My Christian faith was not enough. Unconsciously, I began to get cynical about Jesus answering and meeting all my needs. On a deep level it wasn't happening. I was doing all the right things but I still felt empty.

Then, when I was nearing the age of 30, my world came crashing down. I became seriously depressed, feeling almost suicidal at times, and was admitted to a psychiatric hospital. My anger from the many years of repression shot to the surface; my despair was visible, the horror of living was all around me. At that time I met God, not in church services or though the faces of official religion. No, I'd had far too much of that. Instead, I met God in the kindness of the other patients on the psychiatric ward, those who the world was frightened of and despised. There was life and there was Jesus in the lives of the outcast and I felt at home there. It was a community of pain, but it was also a community of hope, of laughter and of safety.

My recovery was slow but it was happening. During this period God and I were writing different scripts. Unconsciously at first and then more consciously gradual changes took place. One of these was in the area of theology. I questioned old certainties and found them to be untrue. I knew it was no good returning to the old script and the experience of depression left me with a greater openness to others, to suffering, and a new kindness to myself.

I began to see that the old dualism between body and spirit I had held to in my ardent evangelical days was disastrous for me. I went to a Christian psychiatrist with a very clear agenda. How could I live as a Christian and a non-practising homosexual and not fall into depression?' His reply was that I had to look at what was right for me. I thank God for his reply. At the time it set up all sorts of questions and insecurities but, in fact, it was *the* question I had to consider.

The message from evangelicalism was that the body was bad and the spirit was good. I now see that to set one against the other sets up incredibly powerful conflicts, particularly for those people who are gay, but also for many heterosexual people. These conflicts were extremely dangerous and damaging to my emotional health. I have now come to see both body and spirit as part of God's creation and discovered that both are good. What is needed is an integrated balance of body, mind and emotion. I had shut down my bodily and emotional life, frozen it out because I thought it was evil and bad. I had to come out of the emotional deep freeze and experience the light and warmth of God's favour and my own self-acceptance.

I have since come to a position where I believe that gay relationships are good and a gift from God. I now find that I have greater integrity in my faith because I can accept myself as loved by God and loved by, and loving towards, other people. I share my life with a partner who I met in church. One of the great strengths in our relationship is a shared understanding of spirituality. We both have evangelical backgrounds but have now come to love and be nourished by the catholic tradition. Our spiritual strength is found in the Incarnation and in the Eucharist where body and spirit blend and integrate. It is here that the physical world of matter and the non-material world of the Spirit work in harmony. There is no division between the two in God's creative purposes. In the Eucharist there is a unity, wholeness and holiness that nourishes both the body and the spirit.

The church still feels a very unsafe place to be. I wish I could share with my work colleagues in the Church what I had done at the weekend with my partner. For them it is so easy, but I fear that to talk about my girlfriend would have disastrous consequences. It is simple things like this that drive a wedge between the heterosexual world and my own. In my parish church I would love to be able to celebrate the goodness of our partnership. In many ways I live a double life and for the moment that has to be so. But what about integrity – my integrity, the church's integrity? The truth is that you are rewarded if you lie about your sexuality. Honesty is not rewarded. Yet gay people play an active part in church life. If on one Sunday all the gay people in our churches did not attend, there would be many significant gaps in the pews.

7 Playing the game as a gay ordinand

Frank was born in 1963, gained a first degree from Oxford University and a PGCE from London before training as a solicitor. Frank and his partner both come from catholic backgrounds and trained together on a non-residential course. Having been ordained in 1994, he is now priest-in-charge of an inner-city parish.

Looking back, I realise that I became aware of my sexuality at roughly the same time as I became aware of spirituality, around the age of nine. From the beginning, the latter added to my sense of guilt at the former, a struggle which took some twenty years before I reached a happy acceptance of myself as a gay Christian. The ripples, I suspect, will never quite die away completely.

Nevertheless, when I was fifteen, I had thought about a vocation to the priesthood. At Oxford University I went so far as to talk to the Diocesan Director of Ordinands and the Bishop, who both reassured me that being gay was no bar to ordination, and that when I was ready I should present myself in the usual way.

As I waited for sufficient confidence in my calling and pursued other career paths, the 1987 General Synod debate on Sexuality took place. When a local priest asked me why I hadn't considered ordination, I replied, 'Because I'm gay.' I was encouraged by him to believe that despite public pronouncements the Church was tolerant of gay priests who knew how to 'play the game.'

Against the advice of others, I resolved to be open

about myself. I went through a tortuous process by which the Bishop finally agreed that I did not have to commit myself to celibacy provided I accepted 'the discipline of the Church.' Eventually, I found myself on the Southwark Ordination Course (SOC). At my interview for the course, the Principal was sympathetic to my experience, and assured me that I would not be discriminated against on account of my sexuality.

As the course progressed, I found myself able to be more and more open with my fellow ordinands, and on occasion they took up the cudgels for me against homophobic remarks and attitudes from visiting lecturers. Supportive remarks were also in evidence at my final Summer School when a married couple on the course were allocated a double flat whereas my partner and I had separate rooms – a step too far for the staff towards public support for gay clergy. However, we did enjoy performing together at the last night concert 'You made me love you', 'A nightingale sang in Berkeley Square', and 'Let's face the music and dance'. Some visiting Dutch Roman Catholic Seminarians were astonished that this could happen in the Church of England!

Indeed, on one occasion SOC was almost too accepting, when the Principal wrote my Second Year report, and made reference (with my approval) to my then new relationship. The Diocesan Director of Ordinands was a little alarmed, but the Bishop either did not read it, or chose to ignore it. My experience of training as a gay ordinand was a remarkably positive one, and I consider myself extremely fortunate, as I have been in my training parish and beyond.

However, two small irritations remain:

Firstly, that the positive nature of my experience was entirely due to the particular people involved, both in terms of the staff and my year group (eleven women and seven men). To my knowledge there was no policy which could have supported me if any one of those people had wished to make my life difficult.

Secondly, despite the warmth of acceptance and affection which I experienced all the way through my training and to the present day from lay people, colleagues and the hierarchy, I feel I have only ever been tolerated as a second class citizen, and doubt whether any heterosexual Christians (or many gay ones) would dare to consider giving lesbian and gay people equal status and/or equal rights. At the moment I accept this willingly in order to serve God, the world and the Church.

8 Come – follow me

Hervé was born in 1962 in France and brought up in a Roman Catholic family. Having moved to London as a student, he later became an Anglican. Following a career in public relations, he was ordained in 1996, and is now a curate in an inner-city parish.

It never ever occurred to me that one day I would be a priest. As a gay man in a relationship and with an exciting and lucrative career in marketing, there was no reason why I would even consider it. But God and the Church decided differently and to my continuing amazement here I am, a full-time priest in the Church of England. I was born in France in a Roman Catholic family, and went through all the proper stages of Roman Catholic upbringing: baptised when 7 days old, then a Roman Catholic education with first communion when I was 6, confirmation aged 7 and reaffirmation of faith at 11.

As a teenager, like most of my peers I was not particularly interested in God or religion. What attracted me most to church was the organ music, which I loved. But I also remember, when sitting in church, having a sense of not being wanted or included in the Church. I had been aware very early on that I was different, and certainly by the age of 12 knew that I was 'gay' (though I did not know the word for it). For some reason, I felt that the church could not accept my difference. When I attended church, I was there in the flesh but felt like a stranger who would never be able to be integrated in the life of the church and accepted by God. I remember thinking at the time that if God did not want me, then I did not want God either! However, I did continue to go to church because of my fascination with the organ, which I started to study. I would go up to the organ loft every Sunday to help the organist, turning pages, pulling out stops, etc. Church services were merely an opportunity to sit where I wanted to be – at the organ console!

At the age of 17 I moved to a school in London and was very excited to be suddenly away from home. It gave me the opportunity to find out more about myself, and in particular to discover, and read, positive things about the gay movement and gay people at what was an exciting time. I remember the trepidation when I first bought what was then the fortnightly *Gay News*. I felt liberated as I read it. It was like coming home – I was not alone after all! But making the first step to meet people was still a very daunting prospect: I had no problems with acknowledging my sexuality, but was pretty shy and did not, for a long time, have any gay friends to give me the courage to go and meet others.

I then went to college, and eventually did make contact with other gay people through the Gay Soc. This is where I met my first partner – it was good to finally meet others and share experiences, socialising whilst being able to be true to who I was. It was also wonderful at last to meet someone to be with. I had just turned 21, gay sex was legal, and God and the Church could not have been further from my mind at that point! This was when I first started to 'come out' to my family and friends. I was very lucky – my parents, brother, sisters and friends were all supportive, and welcomed my partner. This is not to say that they would not have preferred that I brought a girlfriend home, but they were able to put my happiness first.

After college, I started my career in public relations and was soon busy travelling the globe on behalf of a number of large blue-chip companies. I was working hard and enjoying myself. At that time, I was asked by a friend whether I would replace him as organist in a parish in South London as he wanted to leave. I was keen although did not feel very qualified to go and play in an Anglican church, as I had never attended a Church of England service before. Nevertheless, I did go and meet the vicar and we agreed that I would start. Initially, it was just a Sunday organ playing slot for me, and remained so for over a year. But the vicar knew how to involve people, the congregation was very friendly, and before I knew it, I was a PCC member, organising a small choir, and eventually became a church warden. There was also a sense of something else – not only was I affirmed in a church, but I was affirmed as a gay man. Suddenly I was able to feel a connection with God again!

Some Wantage sisters worshipped in the parish and introduced me to the concept of retreats, which – over time – became very important in my life and spiritual development. In the silence of the convent and the rhythm of the Daily Office, I was able to meet God, able to love God and also able to accept God's unconditional love for me. I was home there too!

One day, I visited some friends in Hertfordshire and we decided to attend the Sunday morning service at St Alban's Abbey. Suddenly and completely unexpectedly, as the liturgy was unfolding, God spoke to me: 'Come, follow me'. I am sure there may be different interpretations to this life-event for me. All I know is it changed my life – it is as if something had turned a switch on and suddenly it was all clear, it all made sense.

It took me a while to try and make sense of the experience, but shortly after, I decided to discuss it with my vicar and offer myself for ordination. He could not quite believe it. He said, later, that he could not have thought of a less likely candidate! He was also pretty unconventional, but even he was not sure how to deal with the gay issue. He had no problem with it, but thought I needed advice from a gay priest, so he sent me packing to someone he had met at a discussion group.

That meeting went well, and I eventually contacted my Diocesan Director of Ordinands. A lengthy process followed, with a number of regular meetings over the course of two years. There was plenty of time for me to read and think through the implications of ordination, and particularly the implications of offering myself as a gay man. By then, my first relationship had come to an end after almost ten years, and I was on my own. I did not want to either deny my past or make promises for the future that I knew I would not be able to keep. I had wrestled with the idea of celibacy but did not feel called to make such a vow, otherwise I would probably have joined a religious order.

Having been an openly gay man since my early 20s, I decided that I would be up-front through the selection process, and that I would either be accepted for ordination as a gay man or I would have to search for some other way in which to fulfil the call from God. With trepidation, I finally went to a selection conference and the moment arrived to have the 'pastoral' interview, the one particularly concerned with personal life and relationships. My interviewer was friendly, and I felt at ease. The question came: 'so, what about girlfriends, then?', to which – after a deep breath – I replied: 'there have not been any girlfriends. I am gay, and I have had a long relationship which is now over'. We talked a bit about my lifestyle as a single gay man, and I made sure to say that, while I was single at that time, there was no way I could make a commitment to celibacy for the future. The rest of the conference was very enjoyable, and it was with even more trepidation that I went back home, to wait for the longest two weeks of my life.

Finally the letter from my Bishop landed on my doormat – my honesty had been commended by the selectors, and I was recommended for training! Needless to say, had the selectors or my bishop been different, I would probably not be here today! The Holy Spirit works in mysterious ways.

My training on a part-time course was very supportive. There were a number of other gay and lesbian ordinands on the course, and the staff were a great source of strength, particularly at the time when gay issues resurfaced at General Synod. I was open with my fellow students, some of whom were very supportive whilst others were a little more circumspect, but I was glad I was able to be 'out' with them. Some people had not knowingly been involved with gay people before, or even thought through the issues, and I think that my honesty helped them to understand that I was just like them.

Ordination and moving into the parish where I am serving my title was the biggest step back into 'the closet' for me. While everyone in the hierarchy is perfectly aware that I am living with my partner (we have now been together almost three years), the vicar's policy as far as parishioners are concerned is that it is better for them not to know.

It may be that some people will never be able to face the reality that a significant number of clergy in the Church of God are actually gay and living in a committed relationship with a partner of the same sex. Many of those are actively (but unofficially) supported by their bishops and their congregations, and all of them continue to offer their priestly ministry to the Church, in spite of the lack of official support and a perpetual threat to their integrity. By now most people are well aware that clergy do have sex, marriage breakdowns, get divorced, even get remarried, and some fall prone to temptations and get themselves into impossible situations. Clergy are not super-human. We are human beings too.

God made me a gay man and God called me to be a priest. I have been ordained in the Church of England as a gay man, and I believe that my role as a priest in the Church is intimately bound with truth, integrity and justice. The only way in which I can exercise my priestly ministry is by pointing to this truth and being able to live in integrity with God and my conscience. I am unable to function as a priest if the Church which has ordained me – in full knowledge – does not respect me for who I am and forces me to be untrue to my own integrity as a human being. I pray with many others for a universal and inclusive church.

9 The lover of all has called

Robert was born in 1964 and after a career in the armed forces was ordained in 1992 after training at an evangelical college. He is now the incumbent of a UPA parish after serving his title in a country town and a second curacy in London.

A bishop of my acquaintance recently met with a group of gay men and lesbians – clergy and lay – in his diocese. It was a meeting of eirenic spirit and of constructive purpose, for he had come to listen to our stories and then to reflect upon what he had heard.

The bishop concerned was no liberal – he was a man part of the Evangelical establishment (although he would probably hate the description). After some of us had shared those stories, of both joy and pain in the church, he was given an opportunity to respond. He began by remarking that what he had listened to was in many ways similar to a Charismatic meeting, with powerful testimonies of God's grace at work in people's lives and of gay men and lesbians reconciling God's call of them to priesthood with the reality of their sexual identity.

I must admit that the connection was a powerful one for me, probably stronger than for the others at the meeting, as I had been part of the culture of Charismatic Christianity for some time. I had trained for ordination at a college closely associated with the Charismatic movement in the Church of England and had served a curacy in a parish where manifestations of the Spirit of God had been a regular part of our Sunday experience. But for me the power of the bishops' analogy was vastly strengthened because what some Charismatics have called the 'Baptism of the Holy Spirit', or the 'outpouring of the Spirit', happened to me in the context of coming out as gay.

My earliest memories of sexual attraction were to men. I can never remember feeling attracted to women, even when in an attempt to 'cure' myself I tried dating women. The problem was I never fancied them!

It was at university that I first began to admit to myself (very cautiously) that I was gay, but it was always in the context of self-loathing and guilt. I was converted at University as well, through the ministry of the university chaplain (with a bit of help from Bishop Maurice Wood and the Holy Spirit) and was nurtured in the faith in a supportive, and relatively open, evangelical community. However, as I look back, I had a lot of guilt and shame to deal with, which some aspects of my Christian initiation compounded rather than helped. No one really ever told me that God loved me – or if they did, I never believed it! Throughout all this time, I was aware of my sexuality, but never really did anything about it (or with it!).

After some three years of subsequent work in my chosen career during which time I totally ignored the inner drives of my sexuality, I was selected for training for ordination. A lot of people talk about some inner vocation, as though God were calling them to ordination. Perhaps surprisingly, given my background and evangelical pedigree, I had no such 'inner voice' or drive. My vocation was entirely pragmatic. Clergy and others had seen in me gifts and talents which they felt would serve

God's Reign if they were used in full-time ministry. The church needed people like me was what I was told. I should consider offering the church my services. It was enough for me and for the selection panel, and I was duly recommended for training by my bishop.

My college was an evangelical one, open enough to permit genuine theological exploration, but closed enough to still have a sort of broad evangelical party line. Liberals and Catholics who trained alongside me often struggled. Despite a number of supportive staff and students, it was not what you might call 'gay-friendly.'

On a two-week placement in Bradford, I found myself sitting through what must have been the most boring evensong I had ever attended. The congregation consisted of five old ladies, a tired and jaded priest officiating, and about twenty ordinands. I cannot recall how it occurred, but I became aware of being totally focused on the issue of my sexuality. I became convinced that God was wanting me to address this issue. I was sure I must talk to someone about it. It sounds rather strange, but it was as overwhelming as that, and the consequences were very frightening. Still, the strength of the experience was enough for me to act and I (heart in mouth) asked a friend if we could go for a drink the next night. In a crowded working class pub in the heart of urban Bradford – in the most macho environment imaginable – I told someone I was gay. My friend listened and was extremely supportive. He promised to be there for me and to pray for me as I explored what it meant. Looking back now, I know he hoped I could be 'healed', but at the time his listening and friendly ear was just what I needed.

Returning to college in the autumn, I spoke to my

Pastoral Tutor. He listened and offered me the resource of a local psychotherapist, to help me think it through. I will always be grateful to my college for being able and willing to finance my therapy, even though it didn't prove terribly illuminating! What I needed was someone else who knew what it was all about to talk it through with. I was still burdened with guilt and could not really reconcile myself to my sexuality.

The next – and most crucial – stage of my journey to self-acceptance came suddenly and dramatically. I can put a time and a date to it, just as many can name the day of their conversion. A fellow ordinand, 'John', someone I knew and respected, came to talk to me about a matter concerning college life (I was student vice-president at the time). Our conversation was followed the subsequent day by the visit of the Rt Revd David Hope as preacher at the college Eucharist. These two events were to prove crucial. I was keeping a spiritual journal at the time. This is an extract:

> *Wednesday/Thursday/Friday:* I think these three days I shall look back on as formative in my Christian walk. 'John' came to see me on Wednesday afternoon. Told me he was gay ... I told him my feelings too. Spent an amazing two hours sharing about it. Since then I have heard so many voices assuring me that my sexuality is part of God's plan for my life. My gayness is a charism! I feel liberated within, as if a huge weight has come off my shoulders. God has said to me that he loves me and wants me to be as I am. I feel as though suddenly *all* my attitudes towards relationships have completely changed. The bishop spoke last night of the 'Kairos moment' – an

event that one can look back on as a key moment in one's faith! Well, I've just had one!! A real sense of God's will for my life as a gay man ...'

Together, these two events proved crucial. As far as I was concerned, David Hope's sermon was for me, and suddenly I knew – above all – that I was loved and that I could love. This is *so* similar to the testimony of many who have experienced 'the fullness of the Spirit' that I call my coming out experience my Charismatic experience – much to the distress sometimes of Christians who tie down the work of the Spirit to speaking in tongues or exorcising demons! A couple of weeks after these amazing events, another member of the college community shared in chapel that he too had been gay and that God had 'healed' him and that now he was happily married. I told my tutor following this that I too was gay, that God had healed me, and I was still gay and very happy about it too!

But equally importantly, this coming out experience, this baptism of the Holy Spirit, had a profound effect on my vocation. Inwardly now – and not just as a pragmatic thing – I knew (in the deep sense of that word) that I was called by God to priesthood, that this was above all else what he wanted for me, and that what had happened to me was to be seminal in my understanding of my calling. Until this point, I had thought that God would allow me to minister *despite* my being gay. Now I knew that he had called me to ministry *because* I was gay. This gift of my sexuality, a gift of the Holy Spirit if ever there was one, was for ministry and mission. My calling was to exercise that ministry and pursue that mission as a priest in the

Church of England – however difficult I or the Church found that!

The Bishop I mentioned at the beginning, after listening to my story and likening his experience to listening to Charismatic testimonies, reminded us that both our stories and those of Charismatic Christians need to be related to the truth of the Gospel as revealed in Scriptures and understood by the Church. They need to be tested.

This is easier said than done, for none of us, as individuals or collectively as the church, can stand apart from our own stories and somehow examine them objectively. Our own experience will always determine our understanding of the truth. This is equally true of our understanding of Scripture. We cannot come to it completely objectively. Fundamentalism and other reactionary movements, such as the Reform group in the Church of England, deceive us and themselves by pretending this is possible. I read the bible and understand the Gospel as a white, working-class rooted, gay, partnered man living in the Northern Hemisphere in London. That will give me insights and blinkers. The Church, however, needs to recognise that she is blinkered too, by sin and cultural conditioning. The only test of truth given to us by Jesus is the test of love. 'By their fruits you shall know them'. I have to ask myself, and I believe as a Church we need to ask ourselves, whether what we do and what we say results in the fruits of justice and love, the destruction of evil and the reconciliation of humanity. In humility, and by the witness of others, I can say that I am sure I am a better person and a better priest now than I ever was in my self-oppressed or *faux*-heterosexual days. There is still much to be done, however, certainly in my life and

definitely in the church!! Being a priest, being gay and having a lover with whom I am sexual are all part of being
me. Each of them is God's special gift. And it is the whole
of me that the Lover of All has called to serve him in his
Church.

10 Called to love

Geraldine was born in 1946 in an evangelical background, became high-Anglican in her teens, and trained at an evangelical college. She is a teacher and an NSM in an urban parish.

I was born to working-class parents in the depths of rural south Shropshire, an only child and the only one of my extended family to have received a higher education and to have 'religion'. I was an intensely devout little girl who was greatly influenced by my maternal grandmother (a women who had worn a Salvation Army bonnet) and by my Pentecostal aunt and cousins. I said my prayers and read my Bible daily from the day I was given my Coronation New Testament – red for a girl!

At Grammar school I fell in love with the RE mistress, who also happened to teach Home Economics. My every waking moment was filled with thoughts of her, but I knew that my feelings were not acceptable. I had overheard the whispers and knew that this had to be my secret.

At fourteen I became an Anglican of the 'highest' possible kind in our part of the world. My first Communion was truly orgasmic, and I believe the link between spirituality and sexuality to be very close, as a reading of some of the mystics will show. Becoming an Anglican coincided with my sense of a call to priesthood. I was told this was not possible but I did not give up. I could be a Deaconess and set out to train, firstly to teach and then to

be a Deaconess. I had not bargained on being called to the
religious life, and in my mid-twenties I decided to test my
vocation in a Religious Community. It was in the rarefied
atmosphere of the convent that I had my first lesbian
experience. I was totally overwhelmed, and tried to
explain the situation to my confessor. I don't think he
knew what I was talking about, and short of drawing him
diagrams, I couldn't find a way of explaining. 'Offer it to
God,' he advised.

Eventually I left the Community and after a while my
convent lover and I set up home together. We supported
each other through therapy and counselling and finally
separated and became our own persons. Meanwhile I had
met another woman who was to be my partner for some
fifteen years. We enjoyed that committed, monogamous
relationship the *Issues in Human Sexuality* commends to
congregations to support. And yes, we did receive unconditional support from our congregation and none the less
so when eventually I was able to realise my calling to
priesthood and go forward for selection.

I was determined to go forward as I was, a lesbian
woman in a committed relationship. If God had really
been calling me for thirty-four years then God was calling
me as I was – a lesbian. I began the long process of selection. At no point did I deny my sexuality or my relationship. My DDO came to tea with me and my partner. My
Bishop knew. I went to the selection conference and risked
all by telling two of the selectors of my situation. I trusted
God, and was accepted, conditionally. I was to be kept
under scrutiny for a year and then would be seen again. I
was not allowed to see the selectors' report but was told
that reference was made to 'problems with relationships'!

For a whole year I lived under the most awful stress, my tutors at college not having any idea why this apparently exemplary student was under review. It was only when I couldn't stand it anymore and confided in the Principal and my tutor that all became clear to them. When I went for my review the two selectors that I had been sent to had no idea why they were seeing me. One of them revealed that they always knew why they were seeing a student but not in my case. I decided that the Church really had had every opportunity to be honest and I was not going to do their dirty work for them anymore and I chose not to enlighten those conducting the review. I got through a second time as my bishop said 'with flying colours, as I knew you would.' He also described me as 'a paragon of orthodoxy'.

I was never sure that at the end of my training I would be ordained; I kept waiting for someone to come up to me and say, 'sorry we can't do it, your story's out'. Even though I have been 'out' for over twenty years I still lived in fear that it would not happen.

The evening before my ordination I was told that AGLO, a campaigning group for Gay and Lesbian ordination in the Church of England was going to protest outside the venue where my ordination was to take place. I was horrified. For years I have worked quietly, tirelessly in the area of sexuality and spirituality and I did not want this group spoiling what for me was the greatest day in my life and in the lives of the other ordinands. At the same time I did not want to collude with the institution and wanted to shout from the rooftops that I was a lesbian called by God and that despite being open throughout the selection process I had been accepted.

The photographs taken of me taken before and after the service tell their own story. The before ones show a terrified woman, and quite rightly so. I shook visibly when the Bishop asked the congregation if it was their will that we be ordained. The split second seemed like five minutes as I waited for someone to shout, 'Yes, all but her' and then name me. After the service, the photographs show a radiant woman, full of the Spirit, fulfilled and happy.

A year later, thirty-seven years of waiting were over when I celebrated the Eucharist for the first time. It was a splendid occasion with all the smells and bells of my tradition, a High Mass with three women at the altar and one in the pulpit, and only one of them a heterosexual. I was surrounded by a packed church representing every part of my life, including many gay and lesbian friends, lay people and clergy. Many of these gay friends expressed sheer joy at being at something which was evidently very mainstream and orthodox and yet so obviously inclusive of all society, young and old, black and white, lesbian and gay. Several who came were not of the Christian tradition, but all were deeply moved by the experience.

I wish that I could reveal my true identity in this essay, but to do so would compromise those who have supported me, and expose them to unnecessary risk. I hate collusion and double standards but this is what a dishonest church compels its most honest members to be party to.

I believe with all my heart that I have been called by God and that I am called as I am, a sexual and spiritual being who is neither disabled nor one who falls short of God's intention and purpose. I believe at the end of the day I will be judged by the quality of my integrity and love. I will face my maker without fear.

11   The struggle within

*Stuart was born in 1947, is from an evangelical back-
ground, is married with children, and was ordained in
1975. He worked for 19 years in the parochial ministry
and is now employed within the NHS.*

'Once you get married it will all sort itself out' was the
advice I was given when I spoke to a Parish Priest, now a
Bishop, about my uncertainty over getting married,
primarily because of the emotional and sexual feelings I
had for my male flat-mate. Coming from a conservative
Anglican evangelical background, I wanted to believe this,
and so I went ahead and got married. My homosexual
feelings were suppressed, although I was constantly being
attracted to other men.

I knew that I was different from a very early age, and in
my early teenage years had a fairly intense sexual relationship with a school friend, but didn't think too much of it
since lots of us were playing around sexually. When Barry
left school, and I stayed on to do 'A' levels, my same-sex
activities stopped too. I suppose I believed that these feelings would go away, and ultimately I would be attracted to
women.

With only two short-lived relationships with girls, and
very little physical contact, I met and fell in love with Sue,
and within six weeks we were engaged. We were married
a year later, and I started training at a well-known leading
Anglican Evangelical College. Never once in my three
years of training was sexuality mentioned. In those days it

was assumed that any evangelical ordinand would be a true-blue heterosexual.

My marriage was happy, we had two children, and on the surface everything was fine. My homosexuality was buried deep within, and to all intents and purposes I was a successful parish priest. My church was growing steadily, and we were described as 'gently charismatic', with other clergy being directed to us to see how it was done.

However in the midst of this success I was having my own personal crisis, and in desperation went and saw my Bishop. I told him there was no scandal, but he needed to know what I was struggling with. By this time I had told my wife. This was the beginning of a process of seeking 'healing'. I went to all the ex-gay counselling organisations that existed at the time, sought deliverance and healing of the memories and attended conferences, but the feelings were still there. Part of the ex-gay's healing process was to have a 'support' group within your church, and so at great cost to myself I shared with close male friends in my congregation, who came alongside and supported me. But it made no difference and I was more mixed-up and confused than ever.

In desperation I turned to the Help Line of the Lesbian and Gay Christian Movement, who provided me with a very professional counselling service. I was helped to accept myself for who I was, and not to deny the reality that I was gay. It was whilst I was in therapy that I met Gordon, another priest, struggling like I was, and a relationship began to form. I was now in such a state, because I wanted to express my feelings for Gordon sexually, but everything within me said it was wrong.

The pressure grew so much that I was on the verge of taking an overdose of paracetamol one afternoon when the door-bell rang. I could see it was my pastoral assistant, and I opened the door, burst into tears and told him 'I want to go to bed with another man'. My pastoral assistant couldn't cope, and went straight to one of my church-wardens; before long the Archdeacon was informed, and a special meeting of the church eldership was called. What hurts me, even today, is that at that meeting, the elders were more concerned with the fact that I wanted to go to bed with another man – *even though I actually hadn't* – than with the fact that I was suicidal. So much for 'sharing one another's burden and thereby fulfilling the will of Christ'.

Fear of disclosure, and my containment of this crisis was uppermost in the minds of many. My Archdeacon gave me three months off, and was himself very supportive. It was suggested I went away, but no financial help was given to enable me to do this, and so there was increasing financial pressure upon the family. Throughout all of this I shared my pain and struggle with my wife, who desperately tried to understand, was very loyal, but also frightened of the future.

After some six months of struggling with our feelings Gordon and I eventually ended up in bed together, and I can only say it felt as if I had come home – it was wonderful and what I had always longed for. A five-year relationship then developed which was, and I think always will be, the most precious, deep, loving, spiritual relationship any human being can have. I loved Gordon with all my being, but it was to come to an end.

The pressure became too much, and my wife gave me

an ultimatum – it was either Gordon or her. I fell apart at having to choose, and everything got very confused and mixed up. I handled things badly, and consequently my relationships with both Gordon and my wife broke up. I didn't know where to turn, for I didn't feel I could go to any person in authority within the church – I would simply be condemned. The emotional pain of losing Gordon was so acute that it was practically unbearable, and on more than one occasion I thought the only way out was to end my life. I saw my doctor and told him I was having to cope with powerful bereavement emotions. He put me on anti-depressants and signed me off from parish life.

Five years on, I am here to testify that I have survived, but this experience has changed me for ever. I was disowned by some of my evangelical 'friends' who I'd talked to about what was happening to me, and I no longer felt comfortable within evangelical circles. I was trying to live with integrity and honesty, but the church would not allow me to do so, and so I lived, being 'economical with the truth'. I struggled with trying to understand a more catholic approach to the faith, but didn't feel I really belonged. On several occasions I have reached the point where I considered resigning my orders.

I don't know what kept me in the church at the time when I was facing all of this. It was 1987 and there was a great deal of negativity coming from General Synod as a result of Tony Higton's motion on homosexuality. My support came from my gay Christian friends and through the friendship and advice of my spiritual director, a Mirfield father. Listening to my thoughts on resigning my orders, he said: 'Stuart, don't you think God knew you were gay when he called you to be a priest?' Of course, with my evangelical background and believing God knew all things, the answer had to be 'Yes'. 'So why do you feel you have to resign your orders?' he asked. There was no answer to that! He also told me to pray a prayer of healing, but not in the evangelical way. He told me to pray every time I celebrated the Eucharist, 'Lord help me to accept myself, as you accept me'. Over a period of eighteen months, that prayer became part of me, and now I know that God accepts me as I am.

'Acceptance' is an important word for gay people, and even more so for gay Christians. For me it became an even greater issue when I had to find the courage to tell my children that I was gay. The biggest hurdle was to tell my 18-year-old son, but I knew one day I would have to. That day came on the 14 February 1996, when I said I needed to talk to him – we sat at the end of my bed for half-an-hour as I unfolded my story. At the end he simply said, 'Dad, you are not telling me anything I didn't already know. Can we have a hug?' Inevitably his response brought me to tears. This has lead me often to ask the question: 'If God can accept and love me as I am; if my son can accept and love me as I am, if all those who I love can love and accept me as I am, why can't the Church?'

The end result of this has been that I left parish ministry some four years ago, and am no longer employed by the Church. For me this was a very important issue, because I felt I could not be paid by an institution that disapproved of me and my life-style. I still go to church, but not on a regular basis though my faith remains very strong.

I believe that as a result of this experience I am a better

person, more understanding and sympathetic to those struggling to live a life of integrity and honesty, but whose life-style would not sit lightly with Christian teaching or morality. By coming alongside and walking with them I believe I am being 'Christ' to them. I am left with a great deal of sadness, and a deep sense of regret that I lost the two most important loves in my life. So far as Gordon is concerned he has moved on spiritually and emotionally, and whilst working in the same geographical area treats me as if that special relationship never existed. I can't do that, and still love him with feelings too deep to express. My wife has stood by me, and I believe still loves me, although I'm not sure why. I still love her, but our marriage has changed, and could no longer be called 'traditional'.

In all of this, whilst I was never disowned by the church authorities, I never really revealed the true me, and whilst I had sympathetic responses, there was no financial help when various courses of counselling were suggested. Let's face it: who could I truly be honest to within the church hierarchy who would have stood alongside me in this struggle of all struggles as far as I was concerned, related to my very existence and identity? I have survived, no thanks to the Church but despite it.

12 People's acceptance of a gay clergy relationship

Nick was born in 1962 and trained for the ministry on a non-residential course following a career in housing. He and his partner live in adjoining inner city parishes.

> Although we must take steps to avoid public scandal and to protect the Church's teaching, we shall continue, as we have done hitherto, to treat all clergy who give no occasion for scandal with trust and respect, and we expect all our fellow Christians to do the same.
>
> *Issues in Human Sexuality*, p. 46

There are around the country increasing numbers of clergy living openly in gay relationships within their parishes. This is greatly to be welcomed, because it means that we can question from experience the assumption made within the Bishops' Report that gay clergy in relationships will cause scandal to their congregations.

This assumption is simply wrong. A profound change has taken place in attitudes to lesbian and gay relationships in the past ten years. It is rarely considered scandalous *per se* for people of the same sex to live together in loving relationships; the causes of scandal for lesbian and gay people are similar to the causes for those in relationships with members of the opposite sex. The Church's fear of providing an active lead in this area has lead church members to experience confusion about their own attitudes in the context of the church. The House of

Bishops in England is culpable in that it has deliberately sought to preserve this confusion rather than providing a lead which welcomes God's love wherever it is found.

The experience of my partner and I, working in parishes near one another in an inner-city area, bears this out. At no time have either of us received any hostility or rejection from any members of our congregations. There are four main factors in our experience.

First, we have found that the congregations of both churches have been welcoming, supportive, and open. For example, invitations to meals from almost all members of both churches are usually extended to both – indeed it causes difficulties when only one can go. Church members are keen to get to know both partners and we are seen as a couple. Surprise is frequently expressed that the hierarchy of the church 'permits' our relationship to continue – surprise and delight that the church on the ground is not as negative as its public pronouncements make it appear. This was most clearly illustrated once when, on learning that John was to move parishes, members of the Wednesday afternoon Bingo Club commiserated with me that I would now have to travel further to see him – 'how will you two cope?' was the question asked.

Second, we have both experienced a huge growth in our faith and understanding of God's love through our relationship – a development which would not have happened if we had been forced to remain secretive and been unable to celebrate our relationship openly. That compassion and love has led to a deeper understanding of our priesthood, which has in turn fed through into the worship and life of the church.

Third, the church has benefited from our relationship,

as it benefits from the commitment of a great many gay clergy – a commitment rarely, if ever, recognised publicly. The fact that neither of us have children means that we can, and do, spend long hours working in the parish and in other associated work – not something which is always easy for clergy with children to do, but certainly a clear example of how gay clergy can give extra time and support to local churches. It is also likely that many inner-city churches would have no priest at all if it were not for clergy without children who are more willing to live in 'difficult' areas.

There is further benefit in that we both offer one another support and advice on day to day situations and tasks – for example, shared sermon preparation reduces duplication and increases ideas!

But the most important factor in our experience of being openly gay and living in a relationship is that without our openness the ministries we carry out would be gravely harmed. At the forefront of everything we do is a desire to be honest and to act with integrity – in other words, to try to practice what we preach. We have found it far more creative to be able to be ourselves within the parish – which means that the people we work among can also be themselves, open and honest, can trust, and can be trusted by us. Without that trust, I can't imagine how I could possibly be a priest and act in a way which communicates God's love: because to be forced to lie about myself would result in a clear lack of trust and openness between me and the parish – hardly a base from which to speak of the love of Jesus.

There is cause for shame within the senior hierarchy of the church that they are willing to try to suppress God's activity out of fear, and to resist the Spirit for the sake of adherence to a concept of human relationships which has little reflection in reality.

13 Growing up with the Church of England

Geoffrey was born in in south London, and lives there still. After unsuccessfully seeking ordination to the priesthood, he now works in senior education management. He worships with his partner at Southwark Cathedral.

There are times when I pause in my headlong enthusiasm for the Church of England. Why is it that I defend and recommend it to my friends, gay and straight, as the best part of the Church in the history of Christendom when, until very recently, it has been unremittingly hostile to my sexuality and, even now, issues at best contradictory messages and, at worst, is mealy-mouthed and hypocritical? Is it only because it's just about the best of a bad lot? Does it go deeper and, somewhere, find a more positive echo in the story of my pilgrimage of faith through forty years? Profound ambivalence towards the Church is not restricted to lesbians and gay men but, for me, the sense that an important part of my God-given personality appeared to be at variance with what the Church has taught has made that ambivalence at times vivid and painful.

Growing up in comfortable south London was somewhat less than challenging. The church of my upbringing was old-fashioned low and seemly. Somewhere in my early teens all that went rather badly wrong with a new, evangelically-minded priest whose arrival coincided with a growing sense that my lack of sexual interest in girls was permanent and that my ever-present sexual interest in boys was here to stay.

Blessed with thoughtful parents, happily free from rigid expectations of how their children should behave, my lack of heterosexual interest was never an issue and, for me, my sexuality was a delight and a source of amusement – I took some pleasure in being different from most other boys. The Church's attitude towards me and my adolescent sexuality was little more that an impertinence. Trapped in an evangelical parish, my 'secret' knowledge gave me a deep mistrust of fundamentalism and a critical distance from born-again Christianity. I sought a faith that I could call my own and I wanted to share something of the religion that my mother valued so highly.

I came out to my parents before I went to university. They had to know that my sexuality was something they had been living with for many years and was, for me, no more odd than my recently married sister's heterosexuality. It was hard work at times for all of us and, needless to say, the parish priest was little better than useless. He was, I suppose, the victim of his tradition and training but was of little consolation to my parents looking for support and guidance. In the autumn of 1977 evangelicalism in Bromley was replaced by the college chapel (gently low), the greater rigours of the Christian Union and, oh praise be! some sexual experience at last.

It now seems strange that I continued to hang around with evangelicals but it was all I knew about and I refused to allow their worries about me stand in the way of my joining GaySoc and engaging in the great undergraduate drive to jettison virginity. It took the death of my agnostic Grandfather to cure me of evangelicalism. I knew that my co-religionists would have Granddad dead as a doornail in their Hell. My choice was between evangelical purity and a God who could not be so narrow-minded – about Granddad or me.

After that it was, in Oxford, only a matter of time before the exotic charms of Anglo-Catholicism were laid before me. I jumped at it. Suddenly the arid plains upon which I had been reared were replaced by the lushness of extreme ritualism and the more lasting growths of catholic Christianity. To my surprised delight I found that here was a religion that satisfied every part of me, spiritually, aesthetically, sexually and, if not always satisfying intellectually, at least it made sense.

Within the year I was a regular church-, chapel- and cathedral-goer and, like so many before me, I had found a boyfriend and a vocation to the priesthood. Boyfriend aside, it all went to pieces in a disastrous ACCM, my return to London, the parental home and the evangelical vicar.

So the first twenty-something years of my life had been spent overlooking or peering around the Church of England's difficulties but not seeking to challenge them directly. I do not believe that my sexuality was directly linked to my rejection by ACCM but, in picking up the pieces, it was clear to me that the mere retreat back into the Anglo-Catholic ghetto was not an option on its own. In those days, even in the early 1980s, it was possible to isolate myself in an almost pre-war world of sexual freedom, gin and lace and pretend that the wicked world of anti-gay prejudice was of no concern. A body such as the Lesbian and Gay Christian Movement (LGCM) would be regarded with as much horror or derision as a vicious and persecuting Bishop.

Having joined LGCM by this time I was, at last, realising that whatever the weaknesses inherent in a single issue campaigning organisation, it was better than conniving at secrecy and hypocrisy that allowed individual security ('Don't rock the boat, dear') at the expense of the frightened and isolated who lived outside the charmed circle.

For most Anglicans, the events of the last fifteen years with synod motions, reports, controversy and the LGCM service at Southwark Cathedral, will be familiar enough. Because lesbians and gays have not been content to save the bishops' blushes and have come out to their friends and colleges, a generation of leaders and 'ordinary' Christians is growing up that knows us as human beings, sharing gifts and needs, and not just as objects of pity and pastoral discipline.

Still, however, homosexual clergy can be cut off from pastoral care in their relationships, relying instead on non-Christian friends or upon the laity for love and support. The whole of the Church of England is not available to lesbian and gay Anglicans. We cannot expect to find warmth and love in every parish – least of all in the churches that boast of these virtues on lurid churchyard posters.

As a gay man I cherish the priests and congregations who will not look askance at my life and my partner. I rejoice that the Church of England retains a breadth and lack of authoritarianism and so, tacitly, permits such acceptance. Yet I mourn the fact of so many lesbians and gay men who, through bitter experience or understandable assumption, spurn organised religion. They have come to believe the cruel untruth that Christianity will not welcome their lives and their loves. I see in their eyes a mix of puzzlement and incredulity that a gay man will even set foot in a church.

My growth in faith and understanding has taken place almost entirely in the Church of England. Here I have discovered the lessons of evangelism, the enduring strength and support of the catholic faith and the abiding love of many, many fellow Christians. No wonder I want to boast of my Church. And yet how many leaders would have countenanced and publicly affirmed any of the gifts I have received through it? How many would feel able to acknowledge the treasures that homosexual people bring to the Church and take from it.

When will our bishops start to have the courage of their convictions, experience and education so that young people can know from an early age that their feelings and their faith do not have to be hidden from each other?

14 Trying to do the impossible

John is priest-in-charge of an inner-city church and in his early fifties. He was ordained in 1971 and comes from a catholic background.

For fifteen years I tried to do the impossible – to fall in love with a woman and get married. My persistence for so long was partly due to ignorance. Surprising as it may now seem, growing up in a pious and puritanical working class culture in the '50s, I wasn't aware that there was such a thing as homosexuality. I now realise that as I entered puberty, all the bits of evidence were there that I was homosexual, but I had no way of realising their significance. There was nobody to talk with about it, no tantalising moments on television to suggest this really existed. I was a shy, withdrawn child, and my few close friends all grew up to be robustly straight – there was no horsing around in the showers at school with them. You can't recognise something if you can't put a name to it. You grew up, and reached maturity, by falling in love with a woman and eventually getting married: that's all we were told. There was no alternative. And so that's what I tried, though I was painfully ill equipped for the task. How I envy the young gay men growing up today, knowing from the beginning that there is an alternative.

Eventually I went right away, as a VSO, and suddenly came alive in a way that I never had before. There were many ways to explain why I was so happy: I was in love with the new country I was living in and I was in love with my job. Now I know that it was because, in a different culture, far from home, I was somehow able at last to be myself and fall in love with a man – love, of such frustrating innocence, but it was love, the real thing. I still didn't admit, or even consciously realise, that the feelings I had for that man were the very feelings my culture told me I ought to have for women. After that interlude of comparative sanity, I went back to searching for my perfect woman. No one can fault me for not trying.

I was trying to cook up a dish I didn't have the ingredients for, and I don't need to tell most people what resulted from that: the sense of failure, inadequacy and incompleteness, and finally the chilling realisation that you are alone and the loneliness is not going to go away. When, in my early thirties, even I realised how futile my quest was and reluctantly began to wrestle with the awful possibility that I was homosexual, feelings of shame, guilt and fear were added. They poisoned everything. I was a missionary, a model priest, admired by all, achieving great things. I came across a remark in an eighteenth-century manual on hearing the confessions of priests: when love is absent from a priest's life, it is replaced with bitter zeal. I had plenty of that, because what I couldn't do was love: I wanted to love, but was frightened and ashamed to. I fled from affection: women's affection because I couldn't meet it, and men's because I was terrified of it. So I made do with bitter zeal, and you can do enough with that to convince people that you are doing a good job and that your life is a success.

I am now so angry because of the waste of those years. I am angry at the ignorance that I was brought up with, angry that it took so long for me to understand who I am and how to love, angry at the stupid, stoic loneliness I endured for so long.

It began to change one day in Penn Station, New York. I was on leave and meeting an American friend. I didn't know that since our last meeting he had started to 'come to terms with his homosexuality'. I was standing, waiting at the wrong platform exit, and he came up behind me and swept me up into a great bear hug. I had never known even that degree of honest, physical intimacy before. I was forty-two years old. We spent the day together, walking the streets, seeing the sights, and he gave me another hug when he caught the train home. My dinner engagement had fallen through and I went to the cinema to pass the time. The film was *Maurice*. I came out of it knowing, for the first time, that what I was, as a gay man, was good, and that the capacity for love, of which I had been afraid and ashamed, was wholesome – I can think of no other word for it – this was the way I could at last be whole. It took another five years before I came out. There were lots of battles still to be fought, especially with myself, but the corner had been turned.

I have no doubt that my homosexuality is God's gift and purpose for me and that I can only use that gift and fulfil that purpose in relationship with others. Sexuality is to do with other people and how you relate to them, not, as used to be said of spirituality, what you do with your solitude. Taking so long to come to that point has left me with anger at the waste of so much that is good within me for such a large part of my life. But I have taught theology and ethics for too long now to be browbeaten by the kind of theology that is peddled around to convince me that homosexuality and its expression are sinful. I have loved and served the church too long to be driven out of it now.

Having put it off for so long, I think I've enjoyed coming out all the more. Coming out is our own special experience, something that straight people can't share and some compensation for all the pain. For me it is the most important conscious experience of salvation I've gone through. I've been freed from shame and I've been given a sense of dignity and worth. I have been freed from lies, lies to myself, lies to other people, a life of pretence. The truth – a truth that comes from God – has set me free. Now, I would say that it is not part of the Christian gospel to encourage people to lie, and where the Church, in effect, does that to gay people, including gay priests, it is sinfully wrong. The one thing I would ask for today is the right to live truthfully.

Some of the real issues

The Bible is not the issue, let us be quite clear about that. Its authority is not at stake. It is not that one side of the debate is faithful to its teaching and not the other. For much of Christian history, the handful of texts that refer to certain homosexual practices have been consistently interpreted to imply condemnation of homosexuality generally. I challenge the authority of the interpretation. For nineteen centuries, on the basis of a greater number of texts far less ambiguous than these, the Bible was consistently interpreted as sanctioning slavery. Yet now, nobody would see that tradition of interpretation as either authoritative or correct, and this is not the only fundamental change in biblical interpretation that the church has been led to.

I challenge the tradition of interpretation regarding homosexuality. In doing so, I believe that I stand with the slaves who, despite the Biblical sermons preached at them, knew that the God of those Scriptures did not condone their oppression. It is an honourable place to stand, one entirely faithful to the Bible. Like them, I cannot believe that either the durability or the consistency of any tradition of interpretation is a guarantee that it has penetrated to the meaning of Scripture, still less to the mind of God.

In the theology of their spirituals, those slaves expressed the truth of the Bible more eloquently and profoundly than the chaplains who in their weekly exhortation, delivered at worship and supported by biblical quotations, charged the slaves to obey their masters.

> Oh let us all from bondage flee, let my people go,
> and let us all in Christ be free, let my people go.
> Go down Moses, way down to Egypt's land,
> tell old Pharaoh to let my people go.

The Bible is not the issue and nor are the beliefs of orthodox Christianity. The words heresy and orthodoxy are bandied about in this debate with increasing frequency, but with little evidence that those who use them with such vigour know which is which. I have never understood which heresy the gay 'lobby' is supposed to be guilty of. Surely, if there is heresy to be found in the present debate it is in the dualism which so undergirds the instincts and arguments of the conservatives.

True Christian orthodoxy, with its dynamic, restless and ultimately hopeful concern for transformation and re-creation, for things as they might yet be rather than things as they are, does not rest easily with social conservatism, and the religious conservatism that it nurtures. Central to the faith as revealed in Scripture is an openness to what God might now be doing to transform a world in need of healing and renewal so that his ultimate purposes might be realised. It is through this perspective that St Paul moves from an apparent acceptance of slavery to a thoroughly Christian rejection of it – that is how I understand the argument of the letter of Philemon. In the debate around homosexuality, there is, tragically, too little concern for that eschatological dimension. We should not only be asking where we are coming from, but where we are going to.

Biblical authority and Christian orthodoxy are not at issue. What is at issue is the honour due to God in his creation. Our present knowledge increasingly makes clear that homosexuality is part of creation. It is not the result of a choice that is wilfully made, rejecting the nature God had given us in favour of a perverse alternative of our own devising. Homosexuals have known what science now tells us – that sexuality is a given. In an atmosphere of greater tolerance we are able to bear witness to that certain knowledge with a clarity we were not previously able to use. I know no nature other than my homosexuality. It is essentially, inescapably, who I am. My inner experience teaches me that I was created this way. This is the raw material I have been given from which to fashion my life.

The real issue posed by this knowledge and experience of the createdness of homosexuality is the stark question – is this what God intended or a mistake he made? We have been classed with others who have been judged to be 'defective' parts of creation – the physically and mentally handicapped, Jews and gypsies. With them we went to the gas chambers, condemned by our failure to conform to what others regarded as normal, to measure up to what they assumed God intended. Now there are those who, in a new twist to an old story, argue that we should be aborted if our sexuality is diagnosed before birth.

Understandably, we are wary of those who assume they know the mind of God and condemn us too readily as a mistake, a failure of God's purpose. Encouraged by society and Church, we have done that all too readily to ourselves. We know the pain of being condemned to live with the devastating conviction that in the profoundest places of our being we are nothing more than a mistake. But if we are not a mistake, we must be what God intended, our sexuality part of his grand purpose. We might speculate on what that may be. Is there something in our nature which contributes to the soundness and completeness of the whole – something only we can give?

Can it be that the very unconventionality of our love is there to stand as a reproach to those who use convention to limit the obligation to love? Convention, society's norms, feelings of class and racial superiority, prejudice, fear of what is different – the list is long and they are used to provide an excuse for those who refuse to love certain people or treat them with dignity. Christians, though under the divine obligation to love even their enemies, discriminate in their loving. They choose between those who they find worthy of their love and those they feel justified in excluding from love's embrace. Has God included us and our unconventional love in his creation as a protest against those sins of exclusion and the narrowing of love's scope?

If homosexuality is part of God's purpose, it is so in its

wholeness. It is to do with love, with relationships and with how people interact. You cannot isolate the orientation from its expression in relationship. Rarely has casuistry plumbed greater depths of absurdity than in the argument that homosexual orientation is not sinful, but its expression is. Sexual orientation is there for one purpose – to be expressed in love.

The capacity for love is not restricted to sexual love, but is nurtured and sustained by sexual love, well practised in relationship. My experience of coming out is similar to many who have finally come to accept their homosexual orientation – it has made all my relationships more loving. At last in my honesty and self acceptance, I am able to love women and heterosexual men in a wholesome way. My homosexuality is the most fundamental tool that God has given me with which to love others.

The capacity to love is not restricted to sexual love, but is nurtured and sustained by sexual love, practised in relationship that is as full, as deep and as complete as possible. In a tradition that honours monogamy this must include the possibility of a faithful, stable, intimate and loving relationship with one other person, two lives intertwined and lived together, the two become one flesh. And physical contact is necessary – when I was, at last, held in another's embrace, I became whole. The hugs, the kisses and the gentle contact of flesh with flesh nurtured and enlarged my capacity for life and for love. They are the very stuff of my humanity, an unalienable right, God's obvious purpose for every incarnate human being.

There is a particular vocation to celibacy for a minority of people, both heterosexual and homosexual. It is God's special grace to them to hold themselves back in reserve from a full physical and emotional relationship with one other person so that their capacity for love may be more widely expressed, but where celibacy is enforced, it will undermine the capacity for love, not enhance it, destroy human life, not ennoble it. The fruits of celibacy forced on those not called to it are the wreckage of human life, cruel desolation, terrifying loneliness and despairing lovelessness. It is impossible to see how those things could ever be part of God's purpose for his creation.

To deny homosexual men and women that 'sexual love, well practised in relationship' is to deny them fullness of life and to disable them in their most fundamental of Christian duties – to love. There are, of course, those who will surmount even that obstacle and live truly love-filled lives. But for most, the denial of the expression of their sexuality in relationship is a denial of the life God intended, for it is to take away something essential of what God has given with which to fashion full and wholesome lives.